WOKE UP
Blonde

Lessons from a
Self-Affirmed Leader

Be Determined!
Move forward with Strength
Live Empowered!
Barbara Ross Miller

BARBARA ROSS MILLER

www.writeabookin31days.com

Woke Up Blonde may be purchased for promotional use.

Please email Barbara@BarbaraRossMiller.com

Library of Congress Cataloging-In-Publication Data

Ross Miller, Barbara

Woke Up Blonde: lessons from a self-affirmed leader/Barbara Ross Miller

First Edition.

ISBN 978-1-5136-3643-6

1. Business Culture   2. Women & Busines

Library of Congress Control Number: 2018905962

Cover and interior design: Stacey Grainger

Cover image: Adobe Stock

Editor: Connie Anderson

Printed in the United States of America

First Edition

Does ultimate success seem unobtainable? Do you feel like you are exerting inertia that's not moving you forward in your career? We often look back to find that we have not progressed as far as our potential. Focus your effort to achieve success!

WITH *DETERMINATION* YOU CAN BUILD THE CAREER-PLANNING *STRENGTH* YOU NEED TO ENJOY AN *EMPOWERED* PROFESSIONAL LIFE. OWN YOUR FUTURE AND...

- Identify your vision
- Recognize your strengths and opportunities
- Seek on-going training and development
- Build the appropriate Strategic Action Plan

Visit me at WokeUpBlonde.com and enter the monthly drawing for a one hour *Strategic Action Plan* mapping session.

DEDICATION

This book is dedicated to my son, Ross,
who gives me purpose and inspiration every day.

CONTENTS

DETERMINATION

決心

Do You *See Me?*

Your eyes go wide, stare
Never seen caramel shades
Skin tight to the face

Chapter 1

Do You *See Me*?

When I walk into a room, especially in a business setting, I count. I count the number of African-Americans in the room. I count the number of African-American women in the room. I count the number of women. Sometimes, I even count the number of single mothers, and I may specifically count the number of East Coast people or New Yorkers specifically. As a minority, it's what you do. And in my more than twenty-five years of professional experience, no matter how big or small the meeting, nine out of ten times, I am a minority in the room. Despite this, I know I count. And so do you!

It's human nature to seek out those who are like you, starting with the obvious similarities. You look for those who can relate to what is *your normal* or what is your experience. You seek your tribe.

A tribe can be defined as a community with shared cultural, social or economic characteristics and most often, the tribe has a leader. Society has recently made a game of the concept of social tribes with various competitive media programs that involve forming sides, voting people off and out of the tribe, and colluding with tribe members to try to achieve a common goal or series of goals. The victor of the contestants in these programs is based on a sole survivor out-smarting and out-maneuvering the competition—and ultimately separating from the tribe in order to win. However, before you hit that milestone, you must be embraced within the circle.

Even as children, we sought to be included in the circle or chosen to be on a side when playing any team-related activity. Our intention was to belong, and not to sit on the outside of that proverbial circle of life. The easiest way to get into the circle—find those that look like you or that act like you, have a similar skill set or, more importantly, similar values as you. Walking into a business meeting can be like walking onto the playground; only the focus is on strategic advancement of the company goals. You want to be in the circle so you can attach, relate, and bond.

Tribal association is critical to fulfilling the inclusion promise of the diversity and inclusion proposition. This diversity and inclusion proposition that you hear many companies and institutions brag of can often be ink on paper and font on web page, *but dissipates where it counts and when you need it most.* If you start the job as a wide-eyed neophyte of business, entering the institution of life known as the contributing workforce, you marvel at the promise of growth and prosperity in a company committed to the equal treatment and non-discriminatory action of providing employment. You commit to the concept of the corporate culture asserted by the talent acquisition team with hope that your tribe is there and waiting. If you are like me, you are excited about many possibilities that a new job or assignment brings. It offers you the opportunity to showcase your skills, hone your talents, and achieve some of the life goals you may have established for yourself early on. You walk through the door with that enthusiasm, accompanied with a level of fear, and a sense of hope that this is going to be the beginning of something awesome.

Employment, having a job, does not constitute a career. Similarly, the creation of a Diversity and Inclusion office, program or officer, does not make for an inclusive corporate culture. Look for both career potential and inclusive culture. And never apologize for looking for your tribe. You are more likely to flourish when you can relate, on some level, to your co-workers. Engaged employees stay productive, have a sense of belonging, and may even feel like there's balance between work life and social life. If you can't identify your tribe, you feel isolated. The tribe helps to establish normalcy for you, and gives you the baseline for what achievement could look like for your circle. At the very least, it will show you how high or low the bar was set before you arrived.

It is critical to get into the circle and be seen. Repeatedly, I have found myself alone on the outside of the circle, wondering why I have not been admitted. It's more disturbing when you get awkward avoidance from those in the circle. We've all been there...eye contact is rare, and conversations happen around you, and no one asks for your opinion. You can feel heat rising up the back of your neck as you look for the opportunity to make your presence known. You notice the few in the room who start to size you up in their heads based on your appearance alone, conscious and subconscious bias making its way to their frontal lobes as their facial expressions serve as a window to their thoughts. "She doesn't belong here. What makes her think she has what it takes to do this job? She must be filling a quota we have to meet. Let's see if she can keep up." This is what I heard in my head from the non-verbal signals in the room. And at this instance I realized that my tribe has not arrived here, and I must become *the heroine of my own story.*

My first business trip to our company's headquarters in Japan was eye-opening. It was a hectic barrage of corporate lessons and life lessons that helped to condition me for the long-haul career voyage. It hit all the marks for being out of my comfort zone. I had traveled outside of the U.S. before, but only with family or on recreation-oriented excursions filled with sightseeing, tour packages, and shopping. This was my first business trip out of the country, something that was more than five years in the making and not without constant revision to the strategic plan to make it happen.

I approached it as an opportunity to demonstrate my strategic prowess in addition to having the good fortune to experience the rich culture of Japan. I had worked with my IT counterparts to formulate a proposal that highlighted the gaps in our current go-to-market planning and to offer a global platform component that could reinvent how we approached the release of our product content. Before getting funding approval from Tokyo executives, I had to build the analysis data to support my hypothesis and equate the results to bottom-line improvements. As a team, we also need to get buy-in from all our U.S.-based stakeholders, including my division president.

I used a small amount of budget to hire a consultant to assist with extrapolating the numbers and building graphical representation of the points we were attempting to make. This was common practice at the company because despite having one of the most intelligent and experienced workforces, the leadership in this office rarely took you at your word. So, it became common knowledge that to achieve a "thumbs up" on your project, you needed an outsider to co-sign on your data. The amount of money spent on consultant-collusion economics could have saved many a job when the layoffs started some years later.

With the agreement of my president and additional agreement from the head of IT, I set out for Tokyo to present to the head of the product divisions and all his direct reports in a meeting where my division president successfully maneuvered to get us on the agenda. I settled into my business-class seat for the 12-hour flight, reviewing my presentation and highlighting my key talking points, double checking the math, and revisiting the slide order. I focused on the little details too, like font consistency, spatial accuracy, and overall visual alignment. We landed on Monday, early evening, having lost a day in flight and time zone conversions. And at the moment we landed, my initiation started. My president and other senior leaders traveling for various meetings, came bustling from their first-class seats invigorated and moving at a pace that I had never witnessed from them before. It was almost as if the Japanese air we were all now breathing had dramatically increased their adrenaline, and everything became a race for life. We rapidly went from walking through the terminal to jogging, my suitcase in tow, with my laptop bag with all my assorted files and accessories, barely strapped in over my shoulder. Additionally, it was winter, and I had coat, scarf, gloves and hat either on my body or shoved in pockets and compartments in my luggage. I obviously had over-packed.

I was the only female on this excursion and chivalry had missed the flight. My mistake was to think they saw me as a woman, when what they saw was another member of the team trying to prove herself. On one hand, I wanted to be viewed like everyone else, but on the reality side of that situation, I wanted help.

Lesson Learned: Executive leadership expects you to acclimate instantaneously.

We floated through the Narita terminal in a rush to catch the next express train to Tokyo, and it wasn't until I sat on the train did my heartbeat start to normalize. Cardio workout for today? Check! Things did not improve upon arrival at Tokyo's Shinagawa station. The group opted to walk from the station versus catch a taxi, given it was only a few blocks away. Having never been there, I fell in line and pushed my belongings out of the terminal and into Tokyo's night air for the uphill trek to our hotel. I longed for a massage and shower but no such luck as we were instructed to return to the lobby in 15 minutes to depart for dinner. By the next morning, I was dragging, dealing with jet lag, sinus congestion and body temperature changes from going in and out of overheated conference rooms to wintry temperatures outdoor. I was struggling with the menu choices and found myself limiting my palette to rice, pastries, and recognizable vegetables.

At the office, I had some downtime before the big meeting and I sat sequestered in a sweltering conference room reserved just for the U.S. travelers to use at their discretion. I introduced myself to colleagues I had previously met only via email or video conference, and I observed how people came in and out of the office areas. The office was monochromatic in shades of gray, and there seemed to be an array of trash disposal options from paper to plastic to aluminum to compost. You name it, there was a trash can label just for it. The employees were also monochromatic, in gray, white and black shades, all about the same height and same weight, men with sweaters or sweater vests and all the women in dresses or skirts, stockings and modest-heeled pumps. They all smiled politely and nodded ever slightly, rarely making direct eye contact.

The meeting was in a different building on a campus a cab ride away. We waited outside the assigned conference room to be notified that it was our time on the agenda. My division president instructed me to look at him for queues on tempo and content, and he would do his best to intercede on my behalf when appropriate. The door opened, and we were escorted into the room by a very petite woman dressed as if she were a throwback from the 1920s, seamed stockings and all. I couldn't, in that moment, recall the last time I wore stockings. No woman in San Diego ever wore stockings. Other than me, she was the only woman in the room. It was a square room filled with all the Japanese men currently in charge of the individual product divisions responsible for everything from engineering to global sell-through within their respective categories. They had their next-in-command with them. The global president they all reported to was seated at the center of the table at the top of the square, and he greeted us with a warm welcome and smile, calling me by name as he remembered our conversations when he had previously served as president of the U.S. business. This helped calm my nerves, and validated that I had made an impression.

I was introduced, and my presentation was projected from the podium positioned at the head of the table, directly behind me. I stood, and the remote was passed to me to control the slides, and I began by reintroducing myself, my role, and the current situation plaguing my team in the U.S. Showing the first slide, I spoke to the bell curve of television product sales in our market, and what the typical peak of the product sales looked like in number of weeks from launch, as well as associated revenue during that time frame. I then went into a chart that showed the promotional calendars of the various retailers we sell through, with their cut-off deadlines for content submission for their newspaper circulars. We consistently missed advertising in these circulars during the first week a product launched because we never had enough critical product data and assets to be included. And while I knew that a large part of this gap was based on trust issues internally, I did not call that out. I knew that product information was not shared because of fear our competitors would somehow get it and beat us to market. But, at this point, we were shooting ourselves in the foot, and I had to articulate that in a way my current audience would understand. I showed the money slide. It diagrammed how much additional revenue potential there was by hitting that launch week circular, and how meeting that target would extend the peak sell-through of the product by several weeks on the bell curve chart. In the one category I was highlighting, it was a significant revenue gain.

The global president stood up and broke into a very serious Japanese-only inquisition that went on for at least 15 minutes. When I looked at my division president to get some sign of what to do next, he whispered, "It's good, let them talk." But the perfectionist in me wanted to finish the presentation I had rehearsed. I had at least six more slides to show, and I had not even reached "the ask." When I glanced over at my president again, he said, "Let it play out." Finally, English was spoken again, and the global leader asked the question "Who is responsible for this data that Barbara came all the way to Tokyo to get?" I scanned the room to see panicked faces on aging men, all of whom had pledged their lives and loyalty to the company. No one spoke, so he asked again. "Who owns this data?" The conversation went back to Japanese and several people talked and tried to explain. Finally, someone stood up to own the responsibility for the flow of product data from the engineering teams, and others in the room nodded and mumbled more words I couldn't decipher. The sacrificial man was tasked with figuring out how to get me what I needed, and I was told that a meeting would be set up while I was there, to discuss and study the situation.

My president stood up and said, "Let's go!" I gathered my stuff and followed him into the hallway, thanking everyone for their time as I exited. In the hall he said I did a great job and that I had gotten their attention and should go into the office tomorrow and try to meet with the point person assigned. Next he said he would see me back home, as he had just enough time to catch the last flight out that evening. And he was gone. And I was left standing in confusion about what happened and what was next.

Lesson Learned: Expect the unexpected, and know how to adjust accordingly.

As I exited the building, I realized I had no clue where I was in relation to the office, my hotel, or the train station. I flagged a taxi and tried to explain where I needed to be, but the driver put me out on the corner, frustrated that I didn't have a map to show him where I wanted to go. We could not communicate with each other. I walked back to the buildings I came out of and saw a sign for a shuttle that appeared to circle all the company campuses in the area. I stood and waited, eventually boarding a bus that took me back to familiar territory near the train station. As I crossed the street to go back to my hotel, a chain of school children crossed in front of me in the opposite direction. They paused, and in amused synchronization, stared at what was clearly the first African American woman they had ever seen live and in person. I wondered about their thoughts as they looked up and down my nearly six-foot frame, turning to look back as I continued across the wide road. I wondered what they knew of black people, and how did they categorize me. Did they *see me*? More importantly, would they ever see me in this homogeneous nation?

I spent the remainder of my trip in meetings with representatives from the product engineering and marketing teams and with the IT team. We diagrammed where the data sets that I needed originated from and how many individual departments had input to the process. I video-conferenced in members of my content team and IT team, and we built a collaborative approach. I left Japan with a "thumbs up," and returned to San Diego to a very excited IT team. I found my tribe.

The IT team members were happy to welcome me into conversations that highlighted how the latest technology architecture could assist my teams in building innovative marketing capabilities. They provided innovative white papers from several vendors that had pitched them upgrades, expansions, and modifications. I became their business advocate, pushing forward the agenda for marketing advancement in an emerging digital landscape. When I stepped back and surveyed where I was, I saw that the IT group was probably the most diverse team in the company. I found my inner geek—and I found a welcoming circle. Yes, I found my tribe.

THE LESSON TO LEARN HERE IS TO:

- Start with the knowledge that you can get into the larger circle, even when your tribe doesn't exist.

- Build a circle within by creating alliances with the least likely suspects–like those who stare the most, question and test you, or are threatened by your presence in the room.

- Draw them closer to you and give them an opportunity to really see you.

- In turn, you will have the opportunity to see them, understand their insecurities, and learn what drives the larger circle of the organization.

- To assimilate with the preexisting culture (some would say you need). I argue that in the absence of an inclusive culture, you need to be strategic.

LEADERSHIP MODELING

1. Identify your top 3 or 4 values (see examples below).

Compassion	Integrity
Honesty	Faith
Success	Happiness
Security	Love
Loyalty	Fairness

    _____

    _____

    _____

    _____

2. List 3 strategic goals to achieve in your current position.

    _____

    _____

    _____

    _____

    _____

    _____

    _____

Yes, This Is My Hair

Yes, this is my hair
You dare peer, squint, ignorant
Of a culture queen

Chapter 2

Yes, This Is My Hair

In seeing me, those who wrote the corporate book of standards, saw my hair first. The texture, complexity and creativity associated with the variety of hairstyles, color and overall appearance of my hair, perplexed most in my office environment. From the always forbidden question, "Can I touch your hair" to the obvious ridiculous comment, "Your hair really grows fast," their ignorance always surprised me.

I was, during the early years of my career, addicted to variety. Relaxed hair, weaved hair, ponytails extensions, and seasonal braiding during the summer months, were part of my repertoire of coif design. Every style was a reflection of the persona I had on the inside that seemed to get suppressed each time I came into the office. This suppression was an act of compliance, not conformance. If my culture had yet to hit the halls of the corporate structure where I was determined to succeed, I had to let it leak out in the most benign form.

Unlike the successful singer and songwriter, India Arie, *I was my hair* and I was desperately working towards being comfortable in my skin. Yet, there was this untold expectation that Arie sung of, this expectation that those in power in corporate environments had of people who looked like me. And while these expectations were unspoken, their implicit bias rang loudly in my head.

There's the expectation of you being the statistical low that makes you an Affirmative Action guarantee, but assumes *you would not otherwise be worthy of the job at hand.* You know this expectation is in play when you find yourself being tested. These tests will be disguised as innocuous queries to see how well read you are or if you can recognize a name dropped into the conversation about a proposed merger of a company next in line to disrupt the industry.

Another expectation is that you are guessing at the appropriate responses needed to generate the steps in the plan because you couldn't possibly know how to create the plan. You can identify this expectation when someone wants to know why you agree with an approach, asked so they can hear you give a detailed argument for your response, despite your response being part of the majority or the same as theirs. You may even be asked some completely random situational question from someone who believes he has the right to interview you now, even after you've secured the job and have been in the role for some time. There's never a logical response to this expectation. This interrogator is most likely someone who exhibits a tendency to be self-absorbed, dare I say arrogant, and you are threatening his world, his circle, the place where he is comfortable.

Feeling comfortable is everyone's desire. For some, it comes with ease. Those are the extroverted personalities that burst into a room or conversation with tons of commentary as they stage a clever inquisition into your life. I'm an introvert who observes and contemplates before taking action or engaging in a conversation, and getting questioned about my background and personal life often puts me on the defensive. Culturally, I grew up knowing that you "mind your own business" and don't ask too many personal questions of people. It was uncomfortable to be exposed to entitled persons whom felt it their duty to know everything about you. Sometimes, I made it a personal mission to be vague in response just to witness how far someone would probe. Questions and comments came from all directions and on all subject matters.

One evening at a business dinner with some Japanese headquarters colleagues, the Japanese global head of brand and design made an audible statement that my new hairstyle was "aggressive." In the thought bubble over my head, I heard myself ask, "Did he just say that?" and I pictured the music stopping in a bar filled with black people as they all turned daggered eyes in his direction. I had my hair styled in a curly Mohawk, with the sides shaved close and tapered in the nape of my neck. I had curls of single thin braids in the top that flowed to the left. I loved it, and received several compliments on how it framed my facial features and made me look both young and New York affiliated.

I was having an out-of-body episode, losing my place in time and having a mental conversation with my inner conscience trying to come to grip with wanting to verbally assault the individual who just commented. I wanted to point out his error, and that he was ignorant in stereotyping me as aggressive. Was it my 5'11" stature, full-figure frame, or African American ethnicity that gave him license? My "in-the-present" self, looked at my boss to read his reaction and ascertain if he heard the words as I heard them. He stood with an uncomfortable smile, urging me nonverbally, to smile too and not dress down this visiting Japanese executive with my words. I nodded to my boss that nod that often only happens between black people as two thoughts connect and become one, and the actions to follow sync. I nodded because even though he wasn't black, most of the time, he got me. I heard a halfhearted laugh come from my mouth, and a forced smile went on my face. Then, my boss said it was getting late, so we should all get some rest before the busy day tomorrow.

Lesson Learned: Be confident and comfortable in your own skin.

Learn to acquiesce, to observe, learn, and thus, build a strategy for advancement. Your ability to identify the gawkers trying to pry into your soul is paramount for survival. It's always good to know the game that's being played. Discern those threatened by your presence, and be aware of the assumptions they have about you based on your hair, or your skin, or the slight accent in your voice, or any other diverse element of your person. Now put on your game face, and take the offensive position of play.

Your strategy, or the plot of the story you are writing, is your offense to the implicit bias you encounter. Look at what drew you to that company and specifically the role and responsibilities of your job. Ask yourself:

- Is your vision to learn one or two specific things that differentiate them within the industry?
- Is the fit more aligned to the mechanics of expanding your skills in your field of expertise?

The two are not mutually exclusive but one should take priority over the other—however you see achievement in your future—so begin to conceptualize what you want.

My vision was to climb as far up that corporate ladder and own the brand and everything associated with it. I wanted to be the creative entity to redefine, reinvent, and reintroduce this historic identity to new consumers to fall in love with. In my role, that meant understanding the components of the brand and how each influenced the other. That was my long-term vision. It would take several connective strategies and constant self-motivation to realize that vision. It drove me to be inquisitive and to be continuously aware of my work environment. I observed and processed all the information that my brain could absorb. I paid specific attention to the interactions between executives and department leaders in order to build the pieces of the puzzle that framed my multifaceted strategy.

Remember that your career is not one-dimensional, and that the triumph of your actions becomes part of the blueprint for your soon-to-be-born tribe.

Your vision is your motivation, and the strategies you create, drive towards that vision. Set realistic and obtainable goals within your approach. Being a corporate CEO may be your ultimate vision, but it is unlikely that it can be accomplished in your first year with the company. Identify your strengths and your learning opportunities, and set your strategic intentions towards leveraging both in order to generate the roadmap for your career. Build a list of learning opportunities, being honest and objective about your current capabilities, and prioritize these as your learning objectives.

Lesson Learned: Know your vulnerabilities and address them before others call you out on them.

Your learning objectives become the foundation for your strategy and should consist of one-to-three short-term goals that can be accomplished in the first third of your strategy timeline. The middle of the planning timeline should be about demonstrating the application of what you learned, and the end of the plan is the time to communicate the results of how you've applied your skills and the value you have contributed. In a two-year vision plan, your learning objectives should be completed in the six-to-eight-month window of that plan.

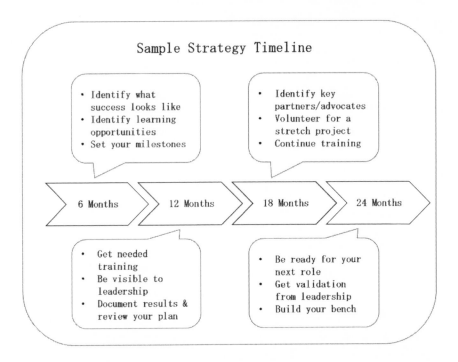

Sample Strategy Timeline

- Identify what success looks like
- Identify learning opportunities
- Set your milestones

- Identify key partners/advocates
- Volunteer for a stretch project
- Continue training

6 Months   12 Months   18 Months   24 Months

- Get needed training
- Be visible to leadership
- Document results & review your plan

- Be ready for your next role
- Get validation from leadership
- Build your bench

Embrace observation and research: they are your friends. Those that provide information about the company history, areas of interest, areas of growth, and areas of failure, can unknowingly aid you in your career climb. Discovery is knowledge, so start with discovery. Who is the keeper of the data you seek, and how do you get face time with these individuals? Let them see you, and build your career circle starting with these colleagues. They can tell the cultural stories of the company and reveal ways you can advance to victory.

LEADERSHIP MODELING

1. Identify your milestones for your Strategy Timeline, looking 24 months ahead.

_____

_____

_____

_____

_____

_____

_____

_____

_____

_____

_____

_____

_____

2. Identify your Learning Objectives for Phase 1 of your Strategy Timeline which should be something you can accomplish in the first four/five months of the plan.

_____

_____

_____

_____

_____

_____

_____

_____

_____

_____

_____

_____

_____

_____

_____

_____

3. Identify two areas of training and development you would like to achieve in the next year.

_____

_____

_____

_____

_____

_____

_____

_____

_____

_____

_____

_____

_____

_____

Did I Give You Permission to Change My Name?

I give you no right
Consent is nowhere for these
Truncated letters

Chapter 3

Did I Give You Permission to Change My Name?

In uncovering the cultural story of the company, you want to plant the seeds of your story along the way. Every good story has a strong heroine or hero, and the author wants you to remember who that is as you learn more about them. The beginning of your relationship with the heroine starts with her name. Everything exists within a name. Some names are unforgettable because they are as unique as the individual. Some names are creative in how they're spelled, which sets them apart, like in the name Lori, also seen as Laurie and even Lorrie. When all is said and done, make sure they get your name correct and understand how critical it is not to confuse it with anyone whose name has any remote resemblance to yours. You want them to *Know Your Name*.

You may be asking why I'm putting so much emphasis on this? I've worked in a sea of Mikes, Jennifers, Steves, Lisas, and Johns. I graduated from high school in a class of eight Barbaras. And, I cringe when people automatically take liberty to shorten my name and associate it to some fictional character from their childhood. I am not a Barb. Nor am I a Barbie. And, should you ever meet me, you would see that now and never have I've been a Babs. I like Barbara, prefer it always and get highly offended when someone I've just been introduced to decides to assume an unauthorized familial casualness with my name. In the world of confirming identity, like Alex Haley, author of *Roots: Saga of an American Family*—my name is Barbara.

One individual decided to test my authority over the team during a critical project delivery. He and his direct reports were tasked with hitting a global deadline for a secret product launch that had been communicated before the team merged. He came to my office to dump the problem in my lap, expecting I would dive in to solve it, letting him off the hook. He stated that his new manager, someone in my direct reporting line, was not around, and that's why he brought it to me. I called a meeting of all his direct reports to understand more clearly what the deliverable was and what it would take to meet it. I then looked at him and told him he had to hit the deliverable, regardless of the overtime needed, and that he and his team needed to give me a full assessment in the morning, a few hours before the deadline. I left them in the room. The next morning, several individual members of his team reported to me that after I left the room this senior manager had referred to me as a "f*#king bitch." That's not my name.

I took several deep breaths and finished my coffee before I picked up the phone to call human resources. I explained what had been told to me and waited for his advice. He said he would open an investigation. I moved forward with my day, meeting with my new disrespectful direct report to confirm that he and his team would achieve the desired launch timing. They had worked out the issues and were good to launch. After several days of investigating and interviewing the team, the HR director confirmed that not only did all the team members confirm what I had reported, but their manager had admitted to what was said. I was asked how I wanted to proceed. My decision was based on not wanting to have that level of disrespect and undermining on my team in any format. He was terminated.

Lesson Learned: It is better to follow due process, versus taking matters into your own hands.

Your name is directly aligned to knowing who you are, what you bring to the party, and demonstrating how you show up in the room. Know the names of the individuals driving strategy, making decisions, and setting the vision within the company. How do they author the cultural story of the company, and what path can you utilize to get an audience with them? Moreover, where is there opportunity to influence and direct the story being created? Recognize that these stories will vary by storyteller, and that everything you hear and learn becomes part of the database you're creating for overall career design within this environment.

Putting technical knowledge and job competency to the side for a minute, the data that you are storing and processing in this cultural database is specific to the political and personal interactions and engagement of the important individuals in the company. This is not a conspiracy exercise. You are not seeking incriminating evidence for some future blackmail opportunity. You are looking for how the puzzle interlocks to visualize the cultural design as it exists in its current state, and to what the hope is of the future image to come. Pay attention to the gaps that may be projected into the business plan for years to come. These missing puzzle pieces are opportunities. Determine how you can help complete the picture.

Lesson Learned: Knowledge is definitely the equivalent of power.

In the company cultures that I've been privileged to work in, the common denominator was often the official origins of the company founders. In a global marketplace, where you are operating across borders, the favorable company will have regional agents built into the workforce to navigate the cultural conversations necessary for the advancement of the company prosperity. It is also commonplace to assign local officers into expatriate roles in regional offices to observe and learn the indigenous norms both in business and social settings. Yet still, some global companies have an innate culture that permeates even the regional locations in a way that overlooks the significant differentiators of the native employees. Sometimes two competing factors exist in this scenario.

First, you need to discern which company cultural norms are significant and career imperative. These are usually corporate vision and/or mission statements that date back to the company's inception, and are part of the genetic code flowing up through the foundation and pulsating through the walls. Some companies build mottos and credos that are printed in handbooks and on plaques, in effort to keep these residual aspirations front of mind. Examples could include the pursuit of excellence. I would interpret this to be a culture that is focused on being the best, winning at all costs, and rewarding perfectionism. Another example could be to foster creativity. This could be interpreted as a workplace where ideation is rewarded, and creative problem solving is encouraged. Many corporate mantras are developed from cultural charters passed along for decades. Sustaining corporate cultures are those that can reimagine their mantras to align with emerging societal and industry evolution.

Second, you need to ensure that neither you nor your career gets lost in translation. Be cognizant of what drives decisions, goals, and accountability in the workplace, and how this aligns to those cultural mantras held in reverence in the halls. If the culture celebrates creativity and rewards disruptive innovation, build that into your strategic plan, and determine to what degree you can enact these qualities in your approach to your job and development. Envision yourself succeeding at this, and it will materialize. If you find that the culture fosters hierarchal arrogance, implicit bias, and ignorant assumptions, you must be determined to prove that those in authority are wrong.

Lesson Learned: Study the cultural norms of the parent organization and what impact they have on you.

Start with challenging yourself to demonstrate *that being different is the positive element of your story and drives you forward.* Don't think in terms of "despite this," but reconcile your vocabulary to state that "because of this," you will succeed. Prepare for battle with hidden bias that you did not author, but that you can erase. Know that you must be better at all of it, and vulnerable enough to understand that you will need help along the way. Set your sights on what you want to actualize. I've built vision boards, and they work. But, you know why you came to the company, and you know what you want to gain from the opportunity. Remember it's an opportunity and not a burden—and every effort you make towards success gets you steps closer to achievement.

LEADERSHIP MODELING

1. Build your Vision Board

Vision Board Basics

✓ Write down what you dream for yourself, and THINK BIG!

✓ Identify 3 goals you need to accomplish to get closer to your dream.

✓ Find visual representation of your dream in words, pictures, and people you admire.
- Build a physical board by cutting out these images and arranging creatively on a board.
- Digital boards can be generated on Pinterest or Instagram.

✓ Hang where you can see daily-or create a screen saver for your device!

DETERMINATION INTENT

- Be the champion of your own story, and create a vision for what you want to achieve within the company.

- Be strategic about your diversity by forming the necessary alliances with those in the company who can move you towards your vision.

- Prioritize your learning objectives to reinforce strengths and develop the skills necessary to succeed.

- Know your name and ensure that others know it, respect it, and associate it with achievement.

STRENGTH

強さ

Angry Black Woman Walking

Attest aggressive
Intense tone predetermined
Black woman's first badge

Chapter 4

Angry Black Woman Walking

*K**now that the process does not come without frustrations.* And
through your determination, you may give off some signals that
have negative connotations in the journey around the diversity board
game. Your serious and introspective demeanor will be misinterpreted as
being angry and isolating. You appear aggressive to most, and some will
have the audacity to verbalize that. To others, you are unapproachable.
After all, you are coming into your self-power, little by little, and
this surge of authentic energy is frightening those who, on day one,
underestimated you completely.

You will be tempted to wield this power like a weapon, cutting down
naysayers and objectors of your obvious talents. Proceed with caution.
Remember, those to whom much is given, much is required. The first
rule of operating at super-human strength in the corporate realm is to
move forward with humility.

To be humble is to be modest about your importance. No one likes the individual that flaunts, brags, or boasts about her or himself. Nor will you be seen in favor by anyone if you appear intimidating to peers, subordinates, and superiors. Be confident without being obnoxious. True talent is best measured in results. Let the inner strength and conviction you have towards progress, manifest itself through your accomplishments. Don't lose sight of your purpose in the company. In addition to your personal advancement strategy, you have corporate, departmental, and individual goals to achieve. Without focus on these, your super power will not matter.

AGAIN, WE MUST REFERENCE THE DATA.

- How is your current role impacting the bottom line of the organization?
- How do you use your super power to work more efficiently and effectively with others striving for the same business results?
- How do you leverage your self-built database to foster relationships that will build on the knowledge and talent you have in order to knock a goal out of the park?
- Where/with whom do you need to partner to get the resources you or your team lack?
- Be deliberate with these alliances—and always be mindful of how they impact your longer-term strategy.

Lesson Learned: Your power is best demonstrated in situations where you can positively influence your audience to stop and notice.

I will admit it took me some time to comprehend how to both focus and leverage my super power. I have that face. What face, you ask? You know the one! That face that says everything I'm thinking just by an expression, including, but not limited to: "You might want to back up from me because I know you didn't just say, do, or contemplate what I think you did." This is the face that automatically puts most people on the defensive. They start to wonder how they offended me. Or they become perplexed by "Why doesn't she like me?" They assume that this face represents someone who's mad at the world or who woke up on the wrong side of the bed. Perhaps, this face demonstrates to some that coffee is one of the daily necessary food groups. The conclusion most people come to when they sum up my facial expressions is: "Angry black woman walking" (ABWW).

Again, I'll cop to and own that I have, on many occasions, worn the ABWW countenance. It usually surfaces when in my head, and most likely later aloud, I call bullshit on something someone has said or done. My "spidey senses" have begun to tingle and my mask has exposed what I really think. It could also signal that I need more information for what was proposed to make the connection in my brain. And, in some cases, it is a sign that you have raised a challenge against me in a way that demonstrates how little you know about me. Now I'm picking up the gauntlet you put in front of me—and coming for you.

Owning your stuff is imperative to building personal strength. You must know what your triggers are in order to build emotional intelligence, hands down the most business essential skill required to succeed. Be cognizant of what pushes your buttons and even more so, how you react when your buttons have been pushed. Regardless of your passion level, you need to demonstrate self-control, maturity, and poise in situations that agitate you at your core. If you need to pause to push the emotion out of view, do that. But don't lose control of the situation or the audience. Isolate yourself briefly if needed. Count to ten, take a deep breath and release the tension with the exhale. Pick up your water and slowly sip while counting it down in your head.

Lesson Learned: Manage your feelings and keep your focus.

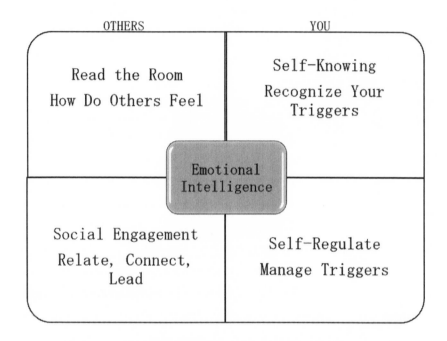

For women, this intrinsic emotional response is expected in situations of stress or opposition: tears. This should be the least likely reaction you have. I have witnessed the strength of women when they calmly articulate their thoughts, opinions, and solutions in weighty scenarios. It can be somewhat chilling when done effectively. It can also be delivered with the authority she owns as a confident leader. Some people will underestimate her acumen because they mistake a soft-spoken female to be weak, vulnerable or ill-prepared. Leverage this and catch the non-enlightened off guard. Vent the emotion in private, in Pilates class or at happy hour, but don't emote in the moment. It's also possible that your reaction could be clouded by your own implicit bias, and you may need to step outside of the perimeter to find a different vantage point to the problem. Be self-aware and adjust as necessary. Conversely, be aware of the emotional retort of others in the room. As a leader, you must both see it and diffuse it. Start by breaking down the facts and removing personal feelings from the discussion. Acknowledge that these feelings exist, but emphasize that they don't belong in the conversation nor should they inhibit the forward motion of the work. Bring the conversation back to the goal, and be collaborative in your direction as you proceed, pausing as needed to calculate the pulse of those involved.

Lesson Learned: Temper your emotional voice with mindful reflection, inspection, and isolation if required.

One of my missteps as a manager occurred when I let myself go too far inside my own head. The person I reported to was in a position that was way outside his comfort zone. He was placed there to both prove himself to be capable of managing a profit-and-loss center, and to potentially prepare him to return in a position of power to his home country of Japan. He was the ultimate micro-manager who had very little people-management skills—and was on his first U.S. assignment. He dictated versus discussed, mandated versus mentored, and was reactionary versus strategic.

This specific lesson for me came after he chose to reprimand one of my team members without involving or notifying me. Returning after lunch, I came back to find him behind closed doors with the young woman. He was accusing her of being insubordinate because she pushed back on a request from one of his other managers, who happened to be a male. I immediately went to enter the office they were in because I needed to understand what had taken place in the hour I had been gone. When I opened the door, I was greeted by a stern look and a gruff, "I will call you in when I'm done." And then he closed the door.

I could feel my blood pressure immediately start to rise as his disrespect slapped me in the face with the callous stare of the closed door. And while I knew he was my boss, I also knew that as a manager, I had a right to weigh in on the treatment of my team, especially if it was something severe, as this was being represented. I went into the hallway and started to pace, ready to pounce, anger escalating in my head. How could he circumvent me? I was her manager, and it should have come to me to address. In my opinion, her response was appropriate, based on the version of the story I got from the rest of the team.

THE QUESTIONS RAMBLING IN MY HEAD WERE:

- Was this a sexist reaction from him?
- Was she supposed to not question the request and just implement it?
- Was he being sexist in not including me?
- Did he not trust my ability to manage the situation?
- Did my ethnicity come into play here?
- What the hell was going on?

When the door opened, he called me in to let me know that he reprimanded her because he felt that it was not her place to question the other manager. She was not responsible for product promotion, just getting the promotion visible on the website. Her tone of voice when she pushed back was inappropriate, he explained. When I inquired why he didn't bring it to me first, he retaliated that he felt it needed immediate attention. And once again, he dismissed me from his office. I still didn't understand, and nothing he told me diffused my anger. I returned to my desk and began to write a complaint letter to the HR Director on how this man had disrespected me, and I enumerated on how in all my years of professional experience, I had never ever been so discounted and disregarded. I copied my manager's boss, our department Vice President, with the hope that my discontent would not go unnoticed.

HR immediately called me and set up time to talk through the situation. While she nodded with what I thought was empathy, her summation of the event was that my employee's behavior was "Maybe because she's pregnant and emotional." Yes, she said that, and I raised my eyebrow in question and concern given I was sitting in human resources. I went to my VP and tried to unravel all the craziness that had occurred in less than 24 hours. He expressed sympathy and told me to be patient as change was a constant, and things in the department would change again. My VP said: Because my manager was Japanese, little could be done, but I should know that my hard work was not going unnoticed.

Later that year he recommended me for a leadership development program to assist me with my career development and to hone my management skills. I came to realize that I was the angry black woman in the office—and I needed to learn to control her. I went through the training. Recognizing your learning opportunities shows maturity and commitment to your strategic plan. Be prepared to reset your steps as you achieve both achieve goals and identify new opportunities.

Lesson Learned: There is always room for growth and development.

LEADERSHIP MODELING

1. Identify at least two key partnerships you can nurture.

_____

_____

_____

_____

_____

_____

2. List two perceptions others have about you.

_____

_____

_____

_____

_____

_____

3. What are your emotional triggers, and how do you diffuse them?

_____

_____

_____

_____

_____

_____

_____

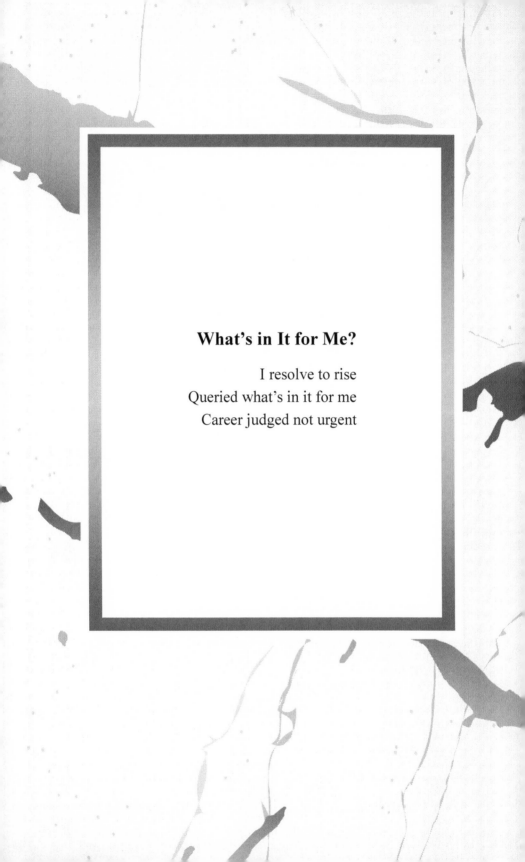

What's in It for Me?

I resolve to rise
Queried what's in it for me
Career judged not urgent

Chapter 5

What's in It for Me?

Training is good. Training makes you stronger. It prepares you for battle, and helps to improve your endurance as you progress on your career trajectory. Along that journey, you will come to the realization that *you have to be the driver and not the passenger if you expect to move forward.* But to see any real evolution in your plan, you have to be able to negotiate, and that means coming to the table with something that's wanted or needed by the other side. Prior to my last promotion with the company, I sat down with a key executive to discuss my insights on the current climate in the building, given the significant number of changes that had occurred over the past several months. During the conversation, he got personal, and asked how I felt about my future with the company, and what I currently had in my purview. I answered honestly and expressed my frustration in not having reached the next level in the company. I felt I had delivered above what was required of my current position, and had added value in other ways through my innovative leadership and staff development and mentoring. I expressed that, per his acknowledgement, I was key talent.

His response to my sharing threw me for a loop. He agreed that I was key to the organization and had driven results. However, he warned that moving up the corporate ladder was not necessarily something I should be rushing to do. After all, he verbalized, once you get to the next level, the opportunities after that are few, and you won't see any movement for a long while. Those jobs don't open frequently at all. He felt it was not a priority within the company at this time to make any additional movements. Again, the voice in my head started shouting at me, and I realized that although being identified as key talent, my reliability kept him from prioritizing my promotion. This was another implicit bias moment, combined with entitlement, since his career steps were often awarded without the same prerequisite qualifications others were told were necessary. The assumption for this Caucasian man was that he had potential, and therefore would succeed. What benefit would it be to him to promote me? A promotion would impact overall operating budget, and had the potential to be a signal for others to come looking for advancement. I was disappointed but not discouraged. I needed to identify the "what's in it for him" proposition.

The company was looking at ways to build loyalty, improve return on investment for programming, and cut operational costs. I focused on these essential business issues, and documented what my teams were doing to target results. Within my span of control, I reviewed my budget, my priorities, and my year-to-date costs to see what could be reallocated and eliminated—in an effort to deliver savings. Adding to my brand story, I gained a reputation as a leader able to affect operational efficiency in my budget, often sacrificing new programs or platform changes to enable more customer-facing yield. I did more in order for me to interject into business conversations, and to not just sit at the table but to participate at the table in a way that had heads turning. I wanted my urgency to be his urgency, and I wanted to convey that while I was loyal, I also knew my worth and understood my competitive advantage as a free agent.

All this time, I had been operating under the assumption that, like him, I had the kind of potential that would push me up that internal ladder. I thought I had the mark, that golden sticker that says, as an effective contributor, I was destined to go the distance. Yet again, I queried if perhaps I was misreading behaviors. I worried that not only had I ingested the corporate Kool-Aid, but it had clouded my vision. I had to step back and survey the terrain. I had to distinguish between my vision and mission—and the company's vision and mission. Were they aligned or had the road forked at some point in my journey? It's important to not get so comfortable with where you're at that you overlook the possibility that you're being taken for granted. Or, in the case of someone of color, you become the corporate trophy, the badge they display when they need to answer the public diversity and inclusion critics.

By this point in my tenure, a tribe of employees of color existed, spread across several campus locations throughout the country. We all connected after arriving at the annual business conference, and were pleasantly surprised that our numbers had significantly increased, being about 3 percent of the total employee population. We created a contact list with office locations and areas of specialty, and we tried to look out for one another through the corporate politics. We mentored each other and hosted each other during business travel, and we shared information on project opportunities and open roles. We supported each other until the financials shifted, promoted by the disastrous 2008 stock market decline, and the divisions and campuses began to vanish in an attempt to bring back the profits from the '80s and '90s. The landscape inside started to mirror the '80s with less diversity in the halls, but the financials refused to follow suit. Many employees vacated to start new opportunities, while others were released, and it seemed that roles were eliminated every six months. A select few of us were hanging on, suspended over the ledge with our nails dug in working to keep our paychecks. We were on that ledge with our Caucasian colleagues too, but the numbers seemed disproportionate. Urgency was everyone's priority as we fought to stay both relevant and valued.

The question that needed answering was what was the true definition of "key talent," and was that definition different for people of color? Did the company actual see people of color as key talent or were we a demographic necessity? I resolved that the correct interpretation of this quandary was both individual and en masse. In our office, there were executives that related to the individual; however, the global entity focused on the numbers. Those numbers broke down in ways that spanned a spectrum, ranging from position description and title, to gender, and of course ethnicity. This was not unlike other companies. However, the ethnicity designation, appeared to stagnate careers—and that was my prevailing plight.

Lesson Learned: Be aware of the reported demographic numbers and indicators for which the company is being held accountable.

Very few individuals fall into a lucrative career without any conflict, obstruction or competition. Favorable navigation relies on one's ability to prioritize learning opportunities, and to leverage both internal and external sources of information. This includes reading the signs within the organization. Pay attention to the power shifts at the top of the house, and determine who's really calling the shots. Current scenarios depicted increased Japanese involvement in our local market. There was obvious pressure to answer to a shift in the consumer spending, becoming more price-conscious, a direct result of a declining stock market and an increased national unemployment rate. The mood in the office was tense and hostile, as everyone defended their role and strived to illustrate their value-add.

Being deliberate about your path puts you in control of your destiny and equips you to answer the call should opportunities avail themselves to you. You must be ready. As a woman of color, you must be more than ready because regardless of how many degrees you have or how much experience you have, you are never evaluated on the same level.

Lesson Learned: Know the credentials of your peer set and your superiors alike.

Recognize that everyone is counting everyone else, their priority formed by their own preference and bias. There's always a hierarchy of consideration, just like there's a pay hierarchy, and *women of color are on the bottom of both.*

LEADERSHIP MODELING

1. Reflect on your Vision Board and write a vision statement for your career aspirations.

_____

_____

_____

_____

_____

_____

_____

_____

_____

_____

_____

_____

_____

2. Create your mission statement for the goals you want to achieve in the 24 months defined on your Strategy Timeline.

_____

_____

_____

_____

_____

_____

_____

_____

_____

_____

_____

_____

_____

_____

_____

_____

3. Do you have synergy with your company's vision and mission?

_____

_____

_____

_____

_____

_____

_____

_____

_____

_____

_____

_____

_____

_____

_____

_____

Silence Is Not Golden

Words absent say all
Unconscious bias voice loud
Equality silent

Chapter 6

Silence Is Not Golden

During one of the many restructures of the company, I inherited additional teams that had previously reported to my boss. I had immediate excitement with these new responsibilities because it appeared to be a move in the right direction and supported my current strategic plan. My team size more than doubled, and my span of control expanded significantly with this change. However, what did not change was my title or position in the corporate hierarchy—so, I asked why.

On an on-going basis, my direct manager routinely scheduled one-on-one time with me for status updates and the like. I found that in the past our conversations were most productive when I came with my own agenda items, and this was at the top of the list. The question went out to my female manager, "Given my new responsibilities, and with the appreciation that they were previously part of your role, will I get the promotion that should accompany the realm of everything you just put on my plate?" There was a pregnant pause, an awkward silence, a deer-in-the-headlights look and a glance down to try to find words that would satisfy my inquiry. Her brow furrowed, and she managed to honestly confess, "I hadn't even thought about it. I'm so sorry."

WTF! I was filled with internal rage as I now stood face to face with this blonde woman, my boss, who achieved her promotion at the onset of her ownership of what I now had. Her promotion was a very strategic maneuver that shielded her from the reporting structure the rest of us were made to suffer through. She was elevated and had direct-line reporting to the CEO, with dotted-line reporting to Tokyo. Her influence was crossing international borders, and she was held up as the example of what women could accomplish in the company. I didn't disagree with the talent she possessed, and I admired the spotlight that surrounded her. Full of hope, I thought it would open doors for me and all the other women trying to break the glass. I couldn't help but notice that now, some two or so years later, the opportunity that was afforded her was not made available to me. This woman had received the proverbial key that gave her access to the inside information and the whispered strategies that the rest of us received in dribs and drabs on an as-needed basis. I wanted that knowledge. I wanted to be on the inside, and I had to figure out why *this was not my time.*

I QUESTIONED SO MUCH IN THAT MOMENT.

- *Was I denied this recognition because I often took on and did extra work without asking for anything in return?* I thought I was showing my potential and proving my worth.

- *Was she illustrating implicit bias by not even considering that, as an African American woman, I deserved the promotion?* No one in the company that looked like me had ever acquired the status that this blonde woman had, and it appeared that this was by design. After all, I was employed by a Japanese company in a male-dominated industry, and to say I was a minority in the company was an understatement. Two other women had gone before her, also Caucasian, but their areas of expertise were not in my purview.

- *Did my achievements not speak for themselves?* I had launched websites and built infrastructure. I had created new incremental revenue sources and united disparate teams to achieve common goals. I had stepped into unchartered territory to execute a strategic plan that spanned cross-functional teams, emerging better equipped to face the competition and build customer loyalty.

Why not me? My fear was that everything running through my mind was in play and I had to determine what, if anything, I could do about it.

It is not uncommon to arrive at a point in your career where you start to compare your own progression to others around you. It can be a dangerous path to go down, but it can also be a necessary journey to take. I had spent my time with the company, head down, focused on getting things done to earn the only paycheck coming into my household to support my son and me. That was my motivation. I charged forward, day after day, to maintain a solid foundation and to be an example for my son. I was appreciative of what my job afforded me, and I needed to stay employed. I had witnessed the reduction of several hundred positions within the company, and I was very conscious of how fortunate I was to be there. However, in this instance, my ego assaulted my brain and synthesized the reflection I thought existed among my colleagues: I was a star! I had to gather inner strength to figure out if there was something wrong with the picture I saw, or if there was something I lacked that I was neither aware of nor had built into my strategic plan.

The political response to my dilemma from the powers that be inside the company was this increase in responsibilities was not a promotion because there was not a position at that level available, and despite the areas being similar, they really were not the same—and the compensation committee did not believe a promotion was warranted. I wondered who comprised the compensation committee, and if there were any people of color on it. What implicit bias bled into that decision? So few people of color were in positions of influence.

Lesson Learned: Don't assume others will advocate for you.

Here I was, feeling isolated in my quest for acknowledgement, and having no tribe or tribe leader associated with this leg of my journey to tap for advice. I needed an external perspective.

Taking an outward glance at the industry, specifically at women of color in my field of marketing, affirmed that while I had bragging rights internally, externally I had not scratched the surface. Missing from my portfolio of accomplishments was the outside recognition that these accomplishments existed. I needed external accolades to bring to the internal table to confirm that my capabilities held value in the larger industry view. It should have been obvious to me, but I completely missed that step. I needed to connect to the industry to be viewed as a subject-matter expert and to secure credibility. I had to generate demand for my voice, my perspective, and my talent. It was essential that my leadership team recognized my market value, and that meant losing the perception *that I would continue to work just to keep my job.* I was building a legacy, and that required building the negotiating and political muscle to take larger risks. My voice had to be more direct, and my story mandated documenting. Absent from my story was a portfolio demonstrating what I had achieved, and how I had delivered quantifiable value.

I REALIZED THAT I—AND EVERY WOMAN OF COLOR IN BUSINESS—NEED TO DO THIS:

- Compile the evidence of my contributions in order to communicate my worth, becoming an excellent tool to use when negotiating salary and promotions.

- Flex my market strength by creating a solid online footprint, leveraging professional social media tools, and associating with professional organizations and communities that give me a varied perspective on emerging industry trends.

- Join the conversation online to further establish my authority on key topics.

- Build my network with colleagues in my field, and connect in person at events and conferences as often as possible.

- Establish executive presence through active participation in industry conferences where case studies, innovative tools, and essential data findings are shared for continuously learn.

- Be consistently present in these learning environments as it keeps me competitive and makes me aware of the talent pool outside of my company.

Lesson Learned: Living your story is not enough if no one recognizes that you're the heroine.

Paramount in telling your story is forging your brand. Your personal brand sets you apart from others and is a mechanism to differentiate yourself in ways that allow you to excel at every twist and turn of the race to advance.

Like a manufacturer specifies what's unique about his product, your personal brand establishes what you bring to the table in the workplace. Your brand should illustrate your values, your expertise, and your methodology for achieving results. These discerning qualities are subjective and intangible, so it's critical that your reputation speaks for itself. Designate your brand qualities, author your story, and reinforce your value proposition by shaping how, when and where to communicate to your internal and external community. Leverage key situations to highlight your brand, and be able to articulate your worth when the opportunity presents itself at events and when introducing what you do. Enlist your tribe to be both your sounding board and your megaphone, singing your praises and brokering integral connections. You are an asset, and your company should recognize and embrace all that makes you special.

My brand represents getting things done with integrity. My super power is keeping things real, and having the courage to respectfully disagree. My philosophy is that *disruption, when the situation calls for it,* is a means to move things forward through creativity and effective collaboration and compromise. I am decisive, resilient, and accountable.

LEADERSHIP MODELING

1. Detail 3 or 4 key accomplishments to include in your portfolio. Remember to quantify your results.

_____

_____

_____

_____

_____

_____

_____

_____

_____

_____

_____

_____

_____

2. List 2 values that are representative of your brand?

_____

_____

_____

_____

_____

_____

_____

_____

_____

_____

_____

_____

_____

_____

3. Create your Brand Statement (50 words maximum).

_____

_____

_____

_____

_____

_____

_____

_____

_____

_____

_____

_____

_____

_____

_____

_____

STRENGTH INTENT

- Be the driver of your career.

- Establish your brand, and know your worth.

- Train to build the muscle you need to stay aware, informed, and ahead.

- Know that company demographics matter, and someone is counting.

- Be mindful of your vision and mission, and how it aligns to the company's vision and mission.

EMPOWERMENT

権限

A "First," Not to be Forgotten

Promotion brings light
Succeeded as corporate first
External press hushed

Chapter 7

A "First," Not to be Forgotten

Change is constant. It is the common denominator of life. Some
change is the result of effort, and some change is the consequence
of conflict or despair. Occasionally both scenarios exist and persist
simultaneously. During advancement, there will be those who champion
and support your movement, and there will be those that circle your
periphery with the hope that they can hinder your ascent. The revelation
you will have is that frequently your blockers will come from within
your tribe.

Being cognizant of transformation occurring in the industry and in
the company, I threw my hat into a risky undertaking to become part
of a newly forming project team tasked with shaking up the traditional
approach to our sales and marketing endeavors. The specific role had
been filled but then vacated as its appointed leader decided to leave
the company. Prior to formally applying for the position, I requested a

meeting with the hiring executive to understand the responsibilities and determine if my background was a fit. Our conversation was effortless, and my subject-matter expertise aligned to his vision for the role. I was offered the job, without formal application, but also at my current title. The question came from me: "Why, if the previous occupant had the title, it was not mine to inherit?" The counter reply was genuine and logical as presented. The incumbent, who took the role and later resigned, brought her title with her, and it was not the original intent to post the role at that level. I contemplated what the best course of action was here, and decided that I needed to ask for what I deserved. I pushed back that if the previous person had the position and the title, there must enough responsibility to warrant it—and I should have the title too. The decision had to go back to committee, and during that wait, I received a call from human resources. She was the highest-ranking woman of color in human resources, and we were peers. We were tribe members. She called to tell me that what I had requested would probably not happen, and that the request was beyond the control of the hiring executive. She told me that he could not justify promoting me, and that I should consider taking the position, minus the title.

How dare she tell me that I should accept less? Why wouldn't she encourage and support me in my effort to even the playing field? I wondered if this was a tactic that HR utilized in their negotiating, and that they had put her up to this call, hoping I would concede and not push hard at this. Regardless, I was disappointed that she would contribute to any behavior designed to oppress people of color. At the end of the situation, I realized that the commentary was owned solely by this woman. She was the oppressor. She did not want to see me, or any other woman of color, succeed before she did. In her role as an HR leader, she was dangerous and divisive, but she had no power over me, and I refused to relinquish my future to her warning. The executive she had deemed ineffective, returned an affirmative response to my request, making me the first African-American woman in the history of the U.S. arm of the company, to rise to my newly appointed and deserved rank.

Lesson Learned: Things, and people, are not always what they seem.

This was my trailblazer moment! It was the reward of owning my voice, my authenticity, and my accountability. I felt that it was a moment to not just celebrate internally by way of company intranet updates and executive announcements, but it was worthy of public and industry recognition. My expectation was that corporate communications would write a press release to give me my due affirmation. That was not the case. And yet again, I questioned the powers that be to ascertain the issue. As one would guess, a Caucasian male was running that part of the organization. He acknowledged that it was great that I had achieved this milestone in my career, and he validated that I was the first. *And then came the "but."* His interpretation of my circumstance was that the company could not risk the potential negative backlash that would come with revealing the company had no other high-ranking African-American women. After all, the company was more than sixty years old, and it was a favorite brand among consumers. Could my announcement impact that? I doubted the accuracy of his concerns, and I desperately wanted to test his hypothesis to prove him wrong, but I knew better. This was a battle better fought another day and in another way.

Lesson Learned: Self-preservation is the rule of survival, but it should not come at the cost of your integrity and values.

I had a deep desire to report this act of deliberate bias to an external authority to bring light to the lack of inclusion I was experiencing. At this intersection of pride and disappointment, I choose to leverage my external network to trumpet my victory. I updated my professional bio to include my new responsibilities, and I delivered the news to several influential contacts and watched as my news hit the circuit of African-American professionals within my sphere. I started to receive invitations to conferences and offers to speak on panels. This community embraced my achievements and rewarded me with visibility and a platform to solidify my brand. And as my recognition grew, my network expanded, as did my view of the diversity and inclusion practices of other companies. These advocates of diversity and inclusion spanned multiple industries, and demonstrated an ability to drive inclusion through shift in their organizational culture. It was not an initiative to be executed and forgotten, it was a systemic mind shift that drove business decisions, resource decisions, and investment decisions. They understood that the diversity of their organization had a direct impact on profitability, and that the composition of their workforce influenced the composition and growth of their customer base. In theory, my company understood this, but in practice, the cultural drivers were derived from Japan. Diversity was not a priority, not from an ethnic vantage point, and it was clearly not something they needed to focus on there. The home office would later declare gender diversity a concern to address in Japan, before turning attention to diversity in other locations.

My promotion was a pivotal moment that could have prompted the U.S. operation to enlist in a more aggressive diversity and inclusion platform, but that was not the case. Business proceeded as usual, and it was up to me to involve others in the mission of addressing the lack of inclusion internally. The methodology I chose and encouraged others to employ, was to bring external examples in for executives and employees alike to view, ponder, and envy. No company is perfect, and often the sense of urgency is ignited through the spirit of competition. By demonstrating what other companies were doing, and how they were succeeding, leadership acknowledged that diversity and inclusion was a competitive advantage for talent acquisition and retention. Several programs were launched to build affinity groups, to establish visibility for diverse managers, and to attract recent college graduates to the company. From appearances, things were moving in the right direction. However, none of it was sustainable because the funding allocation diminished and eventually vanished. Again, the realization of a need for a cultural shift was absent.

Lesson Learned: *Diversity* **was viewed as the responsibility of every manager that had the power to hire and retain staff.**

Unfortunately, what was not clearly disseminated, despite the training, seminars, and keynote speakers, *was that inclusion was everyone's responsibility.*

LEADERSHIP MODELING

1. Reflect on your current tribe and identify anyone who is a potential blocker to your success.

_____

_____

_____

_____

_____

_____

_____

_____

_____

_____

_____

_____

2. Write your professional bio in preparation for speaking opportunities within your industry or your network (300–500 words). Have someone you trust review it and provide feedback.

_____

_____

_____

_____

_____

_____

_____

_____

_____

_____

_____

_____

_____

_____

_____

_____

_____

_____

3. Identify at least one opportunity where you can impact diversity and inclusion at your company.

Impostor Syndrome

Humble and silent
Judgment not worthy, your fear
Impostor Syndrome

Chapter 8

Impostor Syndrome

When you venture outside to find your tribe and gain affirmation for your talent, your worldview expands. It is human nature to make comparisons between your resume and the resumes of the movers and shakers in your industry. You examine all aspects, from length of experience, to affiliations, degrees and other credentials. You Google to read accolades and articles written by and about these stellar professionals. You study their headshots and think how polished and executive they look. In conference and meeting settings, you listen intently to how they seamlessly evangelize innovative industry technologies and spew significant data points that support the latest growth theories. You then let self-doubt creep into your conscious mind. Your brain meticulously dissects everything you've ever done, and your ego begins to painfully and slowly deflate. It is a fear that resonates internally and gnaws at you in professional settings, especially when being introduced with even the slightest pomp and circumstance. *You have Impostor Syndrome.* It happens to everyone at some point in their career, although I would wager that it happens to women and to people of color more frequently than to white males. This is because we spend our lives debunking the stereotypes and pushing boundaries in order to be appreciated for our expertise and brain power. We, as women, are also plagued by "mommy guilt" and perfectionism, and general paranoia that we don't belong or deserve to be where we are.

At the core of the Impostor Syndrome is *the notion of inclusion.* When the evolution of your career is shadowed in corporate quotas and explicit and implicit bias, it hinders the formation of a healthy self-perception. Yet another hurdle is built in your psyche, which confirms the limitations the world wants to envelope around you. What makes you different also isolates you from the proverbial inner circle where ego and confidence live. But confidence, in its authentic form, is derived from the challenges we overcome, from the naysayers we prove wrong, and from the fears we conquer. Impostor Syndrome is just another fear to defeat.

THE FIRST STEP IN VANQUISHING THIS DOUBTING VOICE IN YOUR HEAD IS TO TALK BACK TO IT WITH AFFIRMATIONS OF WHO YOU ARE AND HOW YOU GOT THERE.

- You are a leader.
- You are an example of excellence.
- You are accountable for driving performance and delivering positive results.
- You are a winner.

The second step is to self-promote. Create your "elevator speech" to concisely convey what makes you special. Utilize it when meeting new business contacts so that they remember what you stand for, and why you are important. The final step is to keep true to your brand.

Lesson Learned: When you are empowered to be your authentic self, circumstances fall in your favor.

Shortly before leaving the company, I was offered the opportunity to lead a sales division, which was outside of my marketing discipline. It was an opportunity to step outside of my comfort zone, and to learn a skill set that would not otherwise be afforded me. I inherited the division after the yet another flattening of the leadership layers in the company, replacing two senior leaders who shared this piece of the business. My team of direct reports were a combination of incumbents and reassigned individuals, some of whom had been demoted in title during the restructure. Consequently, previous peers were now subordinate to me—and not happy about it. Our initial start was rocky, but eventually, we functioned as a team. It took continuous communication and building trust to get there. While reviewing employee profile histories, I uncovered that one of my subordinates was actually earning more than me. Yes, he was a Caucasian male. I immediately reached out to HR to see when this discrepancy would be corrected. Again, another inadequate reply to a clear discriminatory situation. Apparently he was grandfathered into his compensation because he came from the old sales organization. This was code for "good old boys" sales organization, based on the inflection in her voice when she told me this. I took the conversation over her head and went to the president to discuss. I was again disappointed in the reaction and response. He didn't seem surprised, nor concerned that this was the case, but he vowed to look at it closer. That investigation came back with the same results, with the added point that my compensation was in line with my peers. I knew that the peer group I was compared to was comprised of the women in marketing. This was the last bit of evidence that I needed in order to know that my time with the company was coming to an end. I was being discounted, devalued, and discriminated against. The breadth of my responsibility was not as vast and prestigious as I was led to believe. I needed an exit strategy.

Lesson Learned: Understand your true span of control.

As I increased my external exposure, I witnessed how my industry peers enjoyed more discretionary spending with their budgets, and this allowed them to have direct impact on a broader and more diverse customer base. *They were touching critical consumer segments in authentic and meaningful campaigns.* My span of control was very limited when it came to external customer reach. The corporate hierarchy I experienced held tight reins on spend-and-budget allocation, and allocated very little to differentiate the customer beyond how Japan defined it. The definition was almost always the same: professional white male between the ages of 18–45. That was always the target we worked to impress, acquire, and retain. Despite the reported and recorded spending power in the Latino and African-American markets, preference was given to neither. No wonder Impostor Syndrome crept in when I traveled to events presented by "Black Enterprise" and "Essence Magazine." The leaders represented at these venues came to impress and engage on behalf of their organizations. Their messages were tailored and insightful, unlike the recycled effort we tried to execute. Our results were a direct correlation of the effort, making it more difficult to justify future spend in these areas. My dialogue with the circle of influencers at these events became increasingly one-sided, and my confidence was often fragile.

In these moments, you need to breathe deeply and stay mindful that you are where you're meant to be, and that you arrived there as the result of your determination and strength.

THEN REALIZE THAT YOU...

- Can build your professional confidence by examining the evidence of your success.

- Were invited into the boardroom and given a seat at the table. Take your seat and get comfortable in it.

- Must use your voice when at the table, and articulate your insights and opinions in a way that demonstrates you are in tune with business imperatives and industry trends.

- Need to be prepared, and trust that you are capable, confident, and empowered to handle your business.

- Must understand that your viewpoint is unique and differentiated from anyone else in the room, and you've labored to build your brand.

- Should work your position to launch initiatives that become part of your legacy.

- Need to deliver the wisdom from your experiences to those who will listen—when possible, and as often as you can. It will carry impact without you knowing and generally without acknowledgment returned to you.

- Must take advantage of mentoring, both formal and informal, as it gives wings and breadth to your power. Help others develop and share your lessons learned with those that can change the future in a positive way.

LEADERSHIP MODELING

1. Create your elevator speech. It should be between 2 to 3 minutes.

_____

_____

_____

_____

_____

_____

_____

_____

_____

_____

_____

_____

_____

2. Write down 3 Affirmations to tell yourself.

_____

_____

_____

_____

_____

_____

_____

_____

_____

_____

_____

_____

_____

_____

3. How will you leave your legacy at work?

_____

_____

_____

_____

_____

_____

_____

_____

_____

_____

_____

_____

_____

_____

_____

Woke Up Blonde

Authentic to self
Aware of implicit bias
Woke up Blonde entitled

Chapter 9

Woke Up Blonde

*M*y parents are part of a generation of adults who spent a
lifetime with their respective employers. They were always
loyal because there were rewards for that loyalty and dedication.
They taught us to do the same, to be steadfast and committed in
our work efforts. It is therefore not surprising that I spent almost
twenty years at the same establishment, pushing through and
hanging in, waiting for the big payoff and reward to come. It was
not an unproductive endeavor, and it afforded me a foundation and
lifestyle to raise a son and instill in him the same moral fibers that
were indoctrinated in me. But over the course of time, *companies
have forgotten that their human capital is their most precious asset.*
They have misappropriated their dissatisfaction with consumer
loyalty into an epidemic of abandonment of the seasoned employee.

My generation is plagued with veteran professionals reinventing themselves out of necessity because somehow they've been devalued in the marketplace. Many have been taken by surprise at this shift in the workforce.

A short time back, I made an active decision to reinvent myself yet again. This time I felt that it was my opportunity to lighten up in my life, and my hair, and embrace my new empty-nest status. It was time to put me first and focus on my well-being, something I had shelved over the years in my efforts to care for everyone else. Prior, I felt I was being selfish when carving out personal time, and I struggled with the concept of relaxation and quiet. However, with the growing awareness of the study of mindfulness, I began looking at meditation practices to assist with clearing my mind and listening in silence. In this silence, I found clarity when reflecting on where I'd been and what I'd experienced. Fundamentally, my mind shifted to the correlation between current cultural awareness, *#TimesUp*, *#MeToo*, and *#BlackLivesMatter*, and those bias situations that haunted my employment history. Mindful, blonde, and *#WOKE* was how I arrived in my new state of being.

The most lucid revelation for me was the continuous rhetoric of how things were "the way they were," with no effort to change. Change is expensive, as is accountability in the face of equality. This is evidenced as the demands for women's rights crescendos while the majority of corporations turn a deaf ear. Who's willing to come to the table and do the right thing to close the gap caused by decades of injustice? This story isn't new, and its ending rarely changes. The headlines would testify that time is in retrograde, and history is recording more inequitable judgement over humankind, particularly those who are disenfranchised. If you choose to be comfortable in this space, know that progress will not occur. I was comfortable and complacent within my cocoon of ambition. That is no longer the option for me, and as such, I see, speak, and act to alter the narrative around me.

When you thrust ahead in constant competition with the portrait of perfection you've generated for your life, you look down and see the treadmill that has entrapped you. It turns, rotates, and cycles forward, and you walk, then jog, then run to catch it, but that can't happen until you to step off. The capturing of that moment gives you pause to comprehend who you've become and what has shaped you. Because you are being still, perceptions fade and truth is prominent and visible. You move beyond living in someone else's truth to owning yours. This has been my experience, and in disclosing my truth, I've understood the complexity of the relationships I've had with my peers and superiors, and with the cultural norms of my company. My discernment of my circumstances have exposed the institutional bias that masked these infractions and slowed the progression of many beyond just me.

Lesson Learned: All that glitters is not gold.

Yes, my most pivotal lesson learned was recognizing that all that glitters isn't gold. As cliché as that sounds, it's applicable to the rhetoric that entitled cultures spew. These cultures are perpetuated by entitled individuals whom, despite their endearing attachment to you and your cause, are not held accountable for that ever-present paragraph in their corporate communications that speaks to equal opportunity employment. Diversity initiatives are diversions that deflect legal actions against the offenders. You need to abandon the role of victim.

TO IGNITE YOUR AWAKENING TO YOUR TRUTH...

- Be present and mindful. Clarity will enter and vision will follow.

- Analyze this vision and accept that imperfection is an element of everyone's truth.

- Own it, and forgive yourself and others for their inherent bias. Without forgiveness, you will transgress.

- Define your future in a manner that aligns to your enlightened vision.

- Be as specific as you can be, and have confidence that everything aligns to manifest your vision and future.

- Stay mindful and still, and know that even in stillness you are in motion, moving towards empowerment.

- Know that setbacks will come, and with them will be lessons. Learn from them, and trust you will emerge stronger and prepared to live your truth.

I've spent more than 25 years in management functions, leading teams and individuals to achieve both business and personal goals. The driving force for my career progression was 90 percent aligned to the expectations of others. I was the first of my siblings to graduate college with a four-year degree, and the first to go on and achieve an advance degree with the completion of my M.B.A. There was pressure to do something with that amount of education, ambition, and exposure. As President John F. Kennedy said, "To those whom much is given, much is expected." This was the impetus of my life—the recording that even today repeats in my subconscious—and it often overwhelms me to deliver on some unspoken promise. It has generated the determination I have to exceed expectations. It has also armed me with the strength to maneuver over, under, and through some of life's daunting obstructions. The immense payoff, after all these years, is empowerment and self-affirmation.

LEADERSHIP MODELING

1. Set aside time to be mindful and still. Note how you felt after completing this purposeful exercise.

_____

_____

_____

_____

_____

_____

_____

_____

_____

_____

_____

_____

_____

_____

2. Identify and analyze your vision—that silent message you heard while being still.

_____

_____

_____

_____

_____

_____

_____

_____

_____

_____

_____

_____

_____

_____

_____

3. List those faults you need to release.

_____

_____

_____

_____

_____

_____

_____

_____

_____

_____

_____

_____

_____

_____

_____

_____

4. Be specific about how you will move forward from here.

EMPOWERMENT INTENT

- Be mindful and still.
- Be forgiving to yourself and others.
- Trust that your vision will manifest.
- Own your truth.

SUMMARY

In life, you often find yourself somewhere unexpected. I believe everything happens for a reason, and each moment presents you with an opportunity to pay attention. My "ah-ha" moment came when I left my job. I recognized I had taken a huge leap of faith. I was very clear about what I would not tolerate any more in my life going forward. I also knew that my lack of work/life balance was negatively impacting my health. I needed to decompress and realign my plan.

My journey has led me to discover that I am more than the labels others have given me or that I was born with. In my upward mobility, I lost myself to choices I felt I needed to make because that was what was expected of me. Now I understand that my sacrifices were made not only for the benefit of my family, but for my benefit as well, and I have begun to take advantage of that. With all that I tolerated and internalized, I had relinquished my voice.

Self-affirmation came as a result of taking inventory of my career. Self-actualization is about living with intent. Don't delay owning your truth and awaking your authentic story. *Thrive with intension and purpose to be a heroine of the story you write for yourself.*

I am Barbara, and I've rediscovered my love for writing and the voice that lives in my head, knocking to come out.

ACKNOWLEDGMENTS

My inspiration and strength comes from my family, immediate and extended. I love and cherish you all. To my mother, thank you for always showing me that windows and doors open because they're meant to. You exposed us to theatre, music and art, and taught us to dance like nobody's watching. To my father, thank you for showing me that hard work and conviction are foundational. You make me always want to succeed. Thank you, Ross, for keeping me sane and always encouraging me by reminding me who I am as your mother, and what I've shown you in life. I love you more! Bert, you are my outside voice, always shouting encouragement, and I love you for it. Thank you Lori, for your consistency in our friendship over the decades that we've known each other. I appreciate you. Thank you, Marlynne for your voice of reason and perspective. It keeps me even.

To my great support circle, thank you for encouraging me to tell my story and speak my truth, especially Tanya, Stacy, and Rosa. I hope you like what I've created, and where I've arrived. To my colleagues, thank you for your understanding and your alliance. To my mentors and professional advocates, thank you for the roads you've opened and the paths you've blazed. To my mentees, I have learned so much about myself in my journey with each of you.

A special thank you to my beta readers, LaQuan, Nicole, and Michael. Your honesty and integrity were priceless in this process. Thank you Jasmine for your insight and advice—and for the introduction to Connie Anderson, editor and life saver during this process. To Larthenia, you have the power of inspiration, motivation and determination.

To all my guardian angels watching over me each and every day, thank you for keeping the fire burning and the light bright in my soul, allowing me to have a voice, even when it's dark. And that special angel always telling me "Be easy on yourself." Thank you.

ABOUT THE AUTHOR

Barbara Ross Miller is a mother, daughter, sister, and auntie. She is a mentor and marketing adviser/consultant with senior marketing leadership and content strategy expertise, and has a proven track record implementing and evolving business strategies to drive revenue growth. Ms. Miller is the former Head of Brand Activation at Sony Corporation of America.

Barbara spent almost 20 years with Sony, and held leadership positions running the Direct Sales organization and Corporate Marketing division for Sony Electronics Inc., including: media planning, CRM, digital content management, and marketing operations teams.

Barbara has been awarded numerous Sony accolades and is listed both as a Top African-American Woman in Marketing and Advertising by "Black Enterprise," 2009 and 2016, Most Influential and Powerful Woman of Diversity by the California Diversity Council, and has been named Trailblazing Mother of the Year by "Working Mother" and Advertising Women of NY.

Barbara volunteers as an executive mentor for WOMEN Unlimited Inc. She is a member of the Links Inc., a community-service-focused organization, and is a Life member of Alpha Kappa Alpha Sorority, Inc. She has a B.A. in Literature and a Master of Business Administration.

Made in the USA
Columbia, SC
05 June 2018